D0602161

Heinrichs, Ann.
Albert Einstein /
2002.
3330520351030
MH   02/26/03

WITHDRAWN

TRAILBLAZERS
the MODERN WORLD

ALBERT EINSTEIN

By Ann Heinrichs

SANTA CLARA COUNTY LIBRARY

3 3305 20351 0304

Please visit our web site at: www.worldalmanaclibrary.com
For a free color catalog describing World Almanac® Library's
list of high-quality books and multimedia programs,
call 1-800-848-2928 or fax your request to (414) 332-3567.

Library of Congress Cataloging-in-Publication Data

Heinrichs, Ann.
   Albert Einstein / by Ann Heinrichs.
      p. cm. — (Trailblazers of the modern world)
   Includes bibliographical references and index.
   Summary: Describes the life and work of the twentieth-century physicist whose theory of relativity revolutionized
scientific thinking.
   ISBN 0-8368-5069-6 (lib. bdg.)
   ISBN 0-8368-5229-X (softcover)
   1. Einstein, Albert, 1879-1955—Juvenile literature. 2. Physicists—Biography—Juvenile literature. [1. Einstein,
Albert, 1879-1955. 2. Physicists. 3. Nobel Prizes—Biography.] I. Title. II. Series.
QC16.E5H382   2002
530'.092—dc21
[B]   2001045630

This North American edition first published in 2002 by
World Almanac® Library
330 West Olive Street, Suite 100
Milwaukee, WI 53212 USA

This U.S. edition © 2002 by World Almanac® Library.

An Editorial Directions book
Editor: Lucia Raatma
Designer and page production: Ox and Company
Photo researcher: Dawn Friedman
Indexer: Tim Griffin
World Almanac® Library art direction: Tammy Gruenewald
World Almanac® Library production: Susan Ashley and Jessica L. Yanke

Photo credits: Corbis/Bettmann, cover; Hulton Archive, 4; AP/Wide World Photos, 5; AP/Wide World Photos/Sotheby's, 6;
Hulton Archive, 7; Corbis/ E.O. Hoppe, 8 top; The Albert Einstein Archives, The Jewish National & University Library,
The Hebrew University of Jerusalem, 8 bottom; Corbis/Bettmann, 9 top; The Albert Einstein Archives, The Jewish
National & University Library, The Hebrew University of Jerusalem, 9 bottom left, 9 bottom right; Hulton Archive, 10
top; Corbis/Underwood & Underwood, 10 bottom; Hulton Archive, 11 top; Corbis, 11 bottom; Hulton Archive, 13; The
Albert Einstein Archives, The Jewish National & University Library, The Hebrew University of Jerusalem, 14; Hulton
Archive, 15; Corbis 16; Hulton Archive, 17; AP/Wide World Photos, 18; Corbis, 19; AP/Wide World Photos, 20, 21; NASA,
22 top; Hulton Archive, 22 bottom; AP/Wide World Photos, 23; Corbis/AFP, 24 top; Corbis/Bettmann, 24 bottom, 25;
Corbis/Underwood & Underwood, 26; Hulton Archive/Ruth Orkin, 28; Corbis/Bettmann, 30; AP/Wide World Photos, 31;
Corbis/Lucien Aigner, 32 top; AP/Wide World Photos, 32 bottom; Corbis/Bettmann, 33; AP/Wide World Photos, 35;
Hulton Archive/Esther Bubley, 36; Corbis/Aaron Horowitz, 37; Corbis/Bettmann, 38; AP/Wide World Photos, 39; Hulton
Archive/Esther Bubley, 40; Corbis/Bettmann, 42; Corbis/Underwood & Underwood, 43.

All rights reserved. No part of this book may be reproduced, stored in a retrieval system, or transmitted in any form
or by any means, electronic, mechanical, photocopying, recording, or otherwise without the prior written permission
of the copyright holder.

Printed in the United States of America

1 2 3 4 5 6 7 8 9 06 05 04 03 02

TABLE of CONTENTS

Words that appear in the glossary are printed in **boldface**
type the first time they occur in the text.

CHAPTER 1

A HERO FOR MODERN TIMES

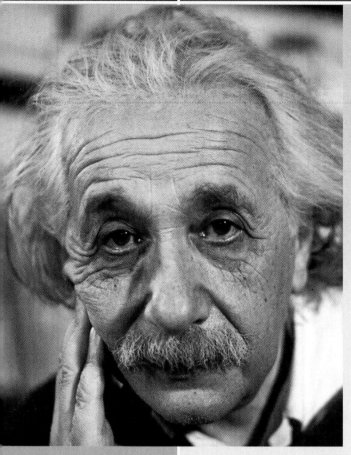

Albert Einstein is remembered for being one of the world's most interesting and innovative scientists.

His face stares out from posters, mugs, and magazine ads—a somber, time-worn face beneath a wild mane of silvery hair. He's a cartoonist's dream—the model for the brilliant but dreamy professor, wrapped in complex thoughts, oblivious to the everyday world.

Although few people really understand his work, Albert Einstein has become a super-hero in popular culture. He was a maverick, an individualist, and an oddball. A self-proclaimed "lone traveler," he ventured far beyond the reaches of the known world and forged a bold new vision of the Universe.

OPENING THE WINDOWS

Albert Einstein has been called the greatest scientist of all time. When people speak of "genius," they point to him as the standard. Einstein gave the world new ways of thinking about space, time, motion, and energy. His discoveries opened the door to the development of television, **lasers**, transistors, computer chips, nuclear power, and space exploration.

He also opened the windows of the imagination. Thanks to Einstein, science fiction took off in fantastic new directions. His theories paved the way for "what-if?" scenarios about time travel, time warps, **black holes**, and voyages to distant galaxies.

Television was invented during Einstein's lifetime, due in large part to his remarkable new ideas.

THE DREAMER

Einstein himself was quite a dreamer, living in a world of his imagination. As a child, he was filled with wonder at things he did not understand. More than a fanciful wonder, it was a serious curiosity about why things happened as they did.

"Imagination," he once said, "is more important than knowledge. Knowledge is limited. Imagination encircles the world."

Einstein is best known for his special theory of **relativity**. It's the notion that space and time are not firm, fixed, and unchanging, but relative—swelling and shrinking with one's point of view. His most popular idea, however, is his famous equation $E = mc^2$. This equation means that energy equals **mass** times the speed of light squared.

Like many of Einstein's concepts, $E = mc^2$ is profound, yet simple enough for anyone to appreciate. Basically, it explains that physical material can be transformed into energy. This principle led to the splitting of the **atom**, which ushered in the nuclear age.

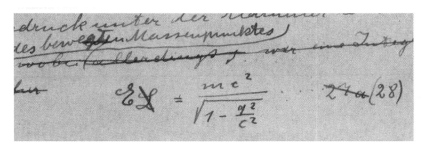

Einstein's famous $E = mc^2$ equation in his original notes

A WORLD RIPE FOR CHANGE

Einstein began his work in the early years of the 1900s. The turn of the century was an exciting time for the budding scientist. Until this time, the field of **physics** revolved around laws set down by Sir Isaac Newton in the 1600s. Newtonian physics had held up to experiments for more than two centuries. His ideas explained why and how material objects behaved.

Now, however, physicists were beginning to see the limits of Newton's laws. They were discovering more and more things that his principles could not explain. These unexplained mysteries were just the stuff that fired young Albert Einstein's imagination. He had to find out how the "huge world" worked, and he was sure it worked in ways that no one had imagined before.

In 1905, when he was only twenty-six, he went far beyond Newtonian physics and proposed astonishing new ways for scientists to see the world. The scientific community did not instantly accept his visions, though. It was another seventeen years before he received the **Nobel prize** for physics.

A MAN OF PEACE

Einstein used his fame to further the causes he believed in. He was a leader among the world's scientists who were committed to peace. Once the atomic bomb arrived, he campaigned for the peaceful use of atomic power.

Einstein was a German Jew, and he was horrified at the treatment of European Jews by Nazi Germany. He joined the Zionist movement to create a Jewish homeland and tirelessly raised money for the cause. Eventually, like many other Jewish scientists of the time, he renounced his German citizenship and decided to leave Europe. In the United States, he continued his crusade for peace, justice, and human rights.

For all his brilliance and fame, Einstein remained meek, mild-mannered, and brimming with childlike wonder. "There are only two ways to live your life," he said. "One is as though nothing is a miracle. The other is as though everything is a miracle."

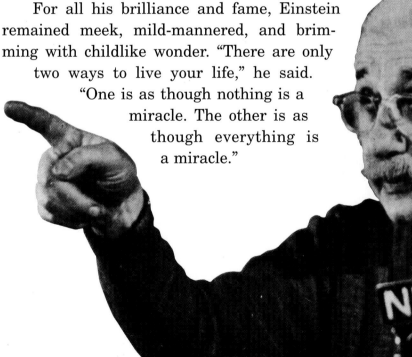

During the 1940s and 1950s, Einstein spoke out against the use of nuclear weapons.

CHAPTER 2

GROWING UP WITH SCIENCE

The German city of Ulm, where Einstein was born

The earliest known photograph of young Albert Einstein

Albert Einstein was born on March 14, 1879, in Ulm, a city in the state of Württemberg, Germany. His parents were Hermann and Pauline Koch Einstein. The Einsteins were Jewish but nonreligious—perhaps as a matter of survival. Jews were not considered German citizens until just a few years before Albert was born.

YOUNG ALBERT

When Albert was a year old, the family moved to the city of Munich. There his father and uncle ran a small engineering plant. In 1881, Albert's sister, Maria, was born. She was nicknamed Maja. Maria remembered Albert's intense concentration when he built houses of cards many stories high.

Little Albert did not begin speaking until he was about three years old. Later he recalled that he didn't want to speak until he could do it right. He practiced putting words together in his mind until he could mentally form whole sentences before saying them.

Pauline loved music and made sure her children had music lessons. By the time he was five, Albert was playing the violin. Later in life, he often picked up the violin and played as he tried to work out scientific problems.

Around the age of five, Albert's father showed him a compass. The boy was intrigued to see that the compass needle always pointed north. "I can still remember . . . that this experience made a deep and lasting impression upon me," he later wrote. "Something deeply hidden had to be behind things."

Albert Einstein and his sister, Maria, in 1884

far left: Hermann Einstein, Albert's father

left: Einstein's mother, Pauline, instilled in her son a love of music.

Albert's parents sent him to a local Catholic primary school. Students there wore military-type uniforms and followed a strict regimen of class work. Albert chafed at the rules. The classes, too, ran against his grain. Doing well meant memorizing mounds of facts. He excelled in mathematics and Latin, but his other grades were mediocre. To his teachers, he was a dreamy, inattentive boy who would never amount to much. His mind was always busy, though.

"There was this huge world out there," he said, "independent of us human beings and standing before us like a great, eternal riddle, at least partly accessible to our inspection and thought. The contemplation of that world beckoned like a liberation." By the age of twelve, Albert was determined to solve the riddle of the "huge world."

At the same time, his uncle Jakob Einstein was challenging his mind. One day, Jakob asked Albert to work out a geometry problem. He was to prove the

As a young boy, Einstein worked to understand the theories of Pythagoras, a mathematician from ancient Greece.

The Einstein family moved to the city of Munich when Albert was a child.

Pythagorean theorem. This was a statement about triangles made by the Greek mathematician Pythagoras in the sixth century B.C. When Albert worked out the proof, he was pleased to find he could establish facts with certainty.

In 1894, when he was fifteen, Albert began secondary school at Munich's Luitpold Gymnasium. It was even stricter than primary school had been. Meanwhile, his father's business was failing, so Hermann moved the family to Milan, Italy. Albert was to stay behind and finish his studies, but he became more restless and discontent than ever with school. His attitude was so negative that a teacher suggested he leave. In fact, the teacher said that Albert's presence destroyed the other students' sense of respect. Albert took his advice, quit school, and made his way to Milan.

Since Albert was so fascinated with science and math, his father thought he should become an engineer. In that case, Zurich Polytechnic (later known as the Federal Institute of Technology) in Switzerland, was

Albert Einstein at age fourteen

The Swiss city of Zurich, where Einstein moved to attend school

A Schoolboy's Plans

While attending school in Aarau, Albert wrote this statement describing his future plans:

My plans for the future:

If I should have the good fortune to pass my examinations, I would go to the [Polytechnic] in Zurich. I would stay there for four years in order to study mathematics and physics. I see myself becoming a teacher in these branches of the natural sciences, choosing the theoretical part of them.

Here are the reasons that led me to this plan. Above all, it is my individual disposition for abstract and mathematical thought, [and] my lack of imagination and practical ability. My desires have also led me to this resolve. That is quite natural; one always likes to do the things for which one has the ability. And then there is also a certain independence in the scientific profession which greatly pleases me.

where he belonged. It was one of the best scientific schools in Europe. Albert traveled to Zurich and took the entrance exam. While he did well on the science and math parts, he failed the foreign-language section.

One of the professors saw that Albert was a promising student. He suggested that the young man move in with his own family in the town of Aarau. There he could study languages at the local school and try the entrance exam again. The plan worked. In the fall of 1896, at the age of seventeen, Albert passed the exam and entered the institute.

Here, too, he was restless and bored, and he often skipped class so he could read other scientific and mathematical materials. He had his own ideas about physics and, with other curious students, was studying and working out physics problems on his own. Fortunately, his friend Marcel Grossman took good class notes. Whenever exam time was coming up, Albert borrowed Marcel's notes and "crammed." As soon as the pressure was off, he was back to his own pursuits.

Albert also began spending time with Mileva Maric, the only female student in his class. She could discuss complex scientific ideas with him, and he liked that. Soon the two were in love. On a visit to his family, Albert told his mother about his feelings for Mileva, but Pauline was opposed to the match. She believed that Mileva was not good enough for him.

Nevertheless, the romance continued. When Mileva became pregnant with Albert's child, she went back to her home in Serbia to have the baby. Albert wrote emotion-filled letters to his sweetheart throughout her pregnancy. At last she gave birth to a daughter, Lieserl. No one knows what became of this child. She may have died in infancy, or she may have been put up for adoption.

In any case, Albert finished his studies and received his diploma in 1900. Now it was time to face the real world and get a job.

A thoughtful Einstein in 1901

The New Father

After Mileva gave birth to their baby, Einstein wrote to her:

My beloved sweetheart!

Poor, dear sweetheart, you must suffer enormously if you cannot even write to me yourself! And our dear Lieserl too must get to know the world from this aspect right from the beginning! I hope that you will be up and around again by the time my letter arrives.

I was scared out of my wits when I got your father's letter, because I had already suspected some trouble.... Is she healthy and does she already cry properly? What kind of little eyes does she have? Whom of us two does she resemble more? . . . I love her so much & I don't even know her yet! Couldn't she be photographed once you are totally healthy again? Will she soon be able to turn her eyes toward something? . . .

I would like once to produce a Lieserl myself, it must be so interesting! She certainly can cry already, but to laugh she'll learn much later. . . .

CHAPTER 3

THE YEAR OF MIRACLES

Einstein's professors would not recommend him for a teaching position. They claimed he simply did not show enough promise, but the truth was they were probably offended by his lack of respect for their process of education. Finally, in 1902, he took a job as examiner at the Swiss Patent Office in Bern. He read the descriptions of inventions and rewrote them clearly for the office files.

A WORKING MAN

Einstein's job may have seemed like a lowly task, but he loved it. Looking back later, he called this the best time of his life. He enjoyed working with the inventors' technical and mechanical ideas. At the same time, the job was not very draining. It left him with plenty of mental energy to work on his own theories after hours.

Einstein's first wife, Mileva, and their sons, Edward (left) and Hans Albert, in 1914

Sir Isaac Newton

Sir Isaac Newton (1642–1727) was an English physicist and mathematician who laid the foundation for modern science. He formulated the law of universal gravitation, which contends that the same force that makes things drop to Earth also holds planets in their orbit. Newton also discovered that white light is a mixture of colors, and he developed the laws of motion that became the basis of physics. He published his theories on motion and gravity in his 1687 book *Philosophiae Naturalis Principia Mathematica (Mathematical Principles of Natural Philosophy)*. It is considered one of the world's greatest scientific works.

He and Mileva finally got married in 1903. The next year, their son Hans Albert was born. Now, besides being a family man and holding a full-time job, Einstein was furiously working on a handful of ideas all at once. Several of those ideas burst forth in 1905, a time known as Einstein's *annus mirabilis*—a Latin term for "year of miracles."

ANNUS MIRABILIS

Sir Isaac Newton had experienced an *annus mirabilis,* too. It was 1665, the year he formulated ideas that laid the groundwork for modern physics. In Einstein's miracle year of 1905, he published several scientific papers in the German journal *Annalen der Physik (Annals of Physics)*. To the scientific community, the papers were absolutely astonishing.

Physicist Max Planck, whose theories about light inspired some of Einstein's work

One of the papers proposed a way to count the number of atoms and **molecules** in a given space. Along with a second paper, it demonstrated that all matter is really composed of atoms. Until this time, scientists had not fully accepted the atomic theory.

In his next paper, Einstein enlarged on physicist Max Planck's theory that light is not a steady beam, but separate little packets or particles of energy, called **quanta**. These particles were later renamed **photons**. Einstein went on to explain the **photoelectric effect**. Scientists already knew that, when a light beam strikes a sheet of metal, **electrons** are ejected, forming an electric current. Einstein's explanation was that quanta of light hold enough energy to knock electrons out of their place in the metal atoms.

Using this idea, scientists eventually figured out how to channel photons and shoot them in a specific direction. This led to the invention of the television. It also paved the way for the photoelectric cell—the "electric eye" that automatically opens doors and turns on streetlights.

THE SPECIAL THEORY OF RELATIVITY

In another paper, Einstein laid forth his special theory of relativity. It presented the earth-shattering idea that space and time are not absolute, but relative. In other words, the theory suggests that measurements of distance and the passing of time change, depending on the position of the observer who is measuring them. Any ideas of "here" or "now" must be measured in the four-dimensional **space-time continuum**. To the three well-known dimensions of length, width, and height, Einstein added a fourth dimension: time.

A popular rumor once said that only three people in the world—or five people, or a dozen—really understood special relativity. It's true that not many people understand all of its mathematical formulas. However, we can look at some of its basic ideas. One is that the speed of light is always the same, regardless of its source or observer. Another is that, as an object approaches the speed of light, its mass increases. No object can move at the speed of light, for then its mass would be infinite.

Relativity also says that a moving clock runs slower than a clock at rest. To state that a different way, time moves more slowly for a moving object than for one at rest. (See The Twin Paradox on page 18.) Yet another relativity principle is that the length of a speeding object becomes shorter the faster it moves.

Einstein at a blackboard explaining some of his ideas

E = MC²: THE DOUBLE-EDGED SWORD

Einstein's last paper of 1905 was a sort of footnote to the previous one. It explains his most famous formula: $E = mc^2$. This equation states that energy equals mass times the speed of light squared (multiplied by itself). This idea means that matter, if it moves fast enough, can be transformed into energy.

In the years to come, scientists were able to prove all of Einstein's 1905 theories and use them—for better or worse. Changing matter into energy proved to be a double-edged sword. Using this principle, scientists were able to split atoms and release the tremendously destructive energy of atomic bombs. This process opened

Some of Einstein's theories led to the creation of nuclear power plants.

the door to the age of nuclear weapons. The same principle, however, generates the nuclear power that provides electricity for thousands of communities. Doctors also rely on nuclear medicine to diagnose and treat a wide range of diseases.

The Twin Paradox

Einstein used the twin **paradox** to illustrate the relative nature of space and time. He spoke of "twin clocks," one of which stays at rest while the other travels away at high speed. Using the human body as a kind of clock, we may apply the same idea to a pair of human twins.

*Suppose Alpha and Beta are ten-year-old twins. Alpha stays home, while Beta boards a space-ship that travels at almost the speed of light. Beta's destination is a planet ten **light-years** away. (One light-year is the distance light travels in one year.) Beta reaches the planet, then turns right around and comes back to Earth—again, traveling at almost the speed of light.*

Back on Earth, Alpha has aged twenty years waiting for Beta to return. Ten years passed on Beta's outward journey, and the return trip took another ten years. For Beta, however, time has passed differently. Beta's inner "clock" slowed way down because the spaceship was moving so fast. When the twins finally get back together, Beta has aged only a couple of months—he is still ten years old while Alpha is thirty!

GRAVITY AND WAR

As Einstein worked day after day in the patent office, he continued to puzzle over the nature of things. Like every science student, Einstein knew the story of Sir Isaac Newton and the apple tree. Newton had been wondering why the Moon stayed close to Earth instead of just flying off into space. There must be some force, he reasoned, that kept pulling the Moon toward Earth.

Einstein spent many hours reading and puzzling over scientific problems.

NEWTON'S APPLE TREE

One day, as Newton lounged in the shade of an apple tree, he saw an apple drop to the ground. Instantly he realized that gravity—the force that pulled the apple to the ground—extended all the way up into space. It must be the very same force that held the Moon in its orbit. This idea became Newton's theory of universal gravitation. It brought physics and astronomy together for the first time, showing that they followed the same laws.

Newton's ideas were revolutionary at the time, but Einstein was sure there was more to gravity. In 1907, he published a paper outlining his principle of equivalence—that gravity and acceleration, or speeding up, are the same force. For example, if you are in an elevator that's speeding upward, it feels as if the floor is *pushing up on your feet*. That pressure, caused by acceleration, is the same as if gravity were *pushing your feet down* into the floor. Realizing this, said Einstein, was "the happiest moment of my life." This idea laid the groundwork for his general theory of relativity.

German troops during World War I

WORLD WAR I

In 1909, Einstein began teaching at the University of Zurich. A year later, he and Mileva welcomed their second son, Edward. In 1914, the family moved to Berlin, Germany. There Einstein became director of the Kaiser-Wilhelm Institute for Physics and a professor at the University of Berlin. That summer, World War I broke out.

Einstein was deeply opposed to the war and criticized Germany's role in it. Many of his fellow scientists shared his feelings. In 1915, he signed a public letter condemning Germany's aggression. This was only the beginning of Einstein's lifelong campaign against war. Needless to say, it did not endear him to German government officials. In time, they would get their revenge against the mild-mannered genius.

Mileva and the boys were vacationing in Switzerland when the war began. The Einsteins' marriage had been deteriorating for quite some time. As Mileva said, "With such fame, not much time remains for his wife." After this separation, they never lived together as a family again. Einstein admitted that he was "not a family man. I want my peace."

Einstein at age forty

In the Eyes of a Friend

The French writer Romain Rolland wrote this description in his diary when Einstein was in his mid-thirties:

Einstein is still a young man, not very tall, with a wide and long face, and a great mane of crispy, frizzled and very black hair, sprinkled with gray and rising high from a lofty brow. His nose is fleshy and prominent, his mouth small, his lips full, his cheeks plump, his chin rounded. He wears a small cropped mustache.

According to Einstein's theories, large objects such as Earth can actually bend space and time.

French writer Romain Rolland was one of Einstein's many friends.

THE GENERAL THEORY OF RELATIVITY

Einstein's main concern, however, was relativity. In his opinion, his special theory of relativity did not go far enough. He believed relativity should apply not only to space and time, but to all facets of the physical world. In 1916, Einstein expanded his earlier ideas about gravity into his general theory of relativity. It went far beyond Newton's theories. Gravity, Einstein said, was not a force. Instead, it was a curved field in the space-time continuum. Any massive body—such as Earth or the Sun—could actually "bend" space and time. This bending behavior is what we have been calling gravity.

Einstein went on to say that it would be easy to prove his theory. Just wait for a total eclipse of the Sun, he said, when starlight can be observed without glaring sunlight getting in the way. Then measure how much a star's light "bends" around the Sun. The results, he predicted, would match the calculations in his theory of gravity—not Newton's.

Understanding Gravitation

To picture Einstein's theory of gravitation, suppose you had a foam-rubber mattress and drew a straight line across it. Imagine a distant star at one end of the line and yourself at the other end watching the star. The line is the path of the starlight on its way to your eyes.

Then suppose you set a bowling ball on the line to represent the Sun. The mattress would sink down. Now the line would not be straight at all. It would curve under the ball on its way from the star to your eyes. According to Einstein, a large mass such as the Sun bends light in this way, so that a star might not actually be located where it seems to be.

Einstein often corresponded with the famous psychoanalyst Sigmund Freud.

Meanwhile, World War I dragged on. Einstein kept up his opposition, passing out antiwar pamphlets around Berlin. Among his **pacifist** friends were the French writer Romain Rolland and the Dutch physicist Paul Ehrenfest. He also carried on a correspondence about war and peace with the Austrian psychoanalyst Sigmund Freud. When the war ended in 1918, Einstein was overjoyed but perhaps a little shortsighted. He thought that Germany had learned a lesson and was finished with militarism for good. Little did he know that Germany's worst aggression was yet to come.

CHAPTER 5

WORLD FAME

A view of the Sun during a solar eclipse

After he attained his fame, Einstein had to deal with constant attention from reporters.

Scientists finally had a chance to test Einstein's general theory of relativity in 1919. Researchers from the Royal Astronomical Society of London traveled to the island of Príncipe off the coast of West Africa. From there they had an ideal view of the Sun during a total eclipse. They measured the light emitted from a certain star and found that its light was deflected, or bent, by just the amount that Einstein had predicted.

A STAR IS BORN

On November 7, 1919, the *London Times* proclaimed the news:

REVOLUTION IN SCIENCE
New Theory of the Universe
Newtonian Ideas Overthrown

The society's announcement hit newspapers around the world. Einstein was declared the greatest genius on the face of the Earth. Now his fame spread far beyond the scientific community. Although most people could not really understand his ideas, the Einstein name became a household word—and a symbol for brilliance.

Einstein was befuddled by his instant fame. After all, he had been publishing his theories for almost two decades. Now he was hounded by reporters, intellectuals, and curiosity-seekers hungry to know his every thought, word, and deed. "Why is it that nobody understands me and everybody likes me?" he wondered.

WIVES AND LOVERS

Einstein's personal life took a turn at this time. His separation from Mileva during the war had turned into a permanent split. In 1919, he divorced her and married his second cousin Elsa Einstein Löwenthall. Elsa was a widow with two grown daughters, Ilse and Margot.

Mileva's knowledge of science had been a big attraction for Einstein at first. Some historians suggest that she may have contributed to his relativity theories. He once wrote to her, "How happy and proud I will be when both of us together will have brought our work on relative motion to a successful end." Clearly, his feelings had changed over the years. After marrying Elsa, Einstein wrote, "I'm glad my wife doesn't know any science. My first wife did."

The two wives did share certain problems, though. Both had to deal with Einstein's female admirers, some of whom were more than passing interests for the celebrity scientist. Elsa, like Mileva, often suffered the pain of his relationships with other women. However, she chose to brush them off. A man of such brilliance, she said, was bound to have a few flaws.

A Humble Soul

These are some of Einstein's thoughts about himself:

- *I have no particular talent. I am merely inquisitive.*

- *It's not that I'm so smart. It's just that I stay with the problems longer.*

- *If I had my life to live over again, I'd be a plumber.*

- *My life is a simple thing that would interest no one. It is a known fact that I was born, and that is all that is necessary.*

Einstein and his second wife, Elsa, in 1921

Anti-Semitism, or hostility to Jews, was on the rise in Germany, and Einstein was an easy target. Some people attacked his "Jewish physics" and called his relativity theories "radical Jewish ideas." At the same time, Jews in Europe were calling for a nation of their own. Their campaign for a homeland was called Zionism, after Zion, the mount on which the temple in Jerusalem once stood. The Zionist movement appealed to Einstein, and he began to support it publicly. That only added fuel to the growing hatred of his opponents.

Einstein's foes were quick to point out that he was not a "real Jew" because he didn't practice his religion. He himself said, "Much as I feel myself a Jew, I feel far removed from traditional religious forms." Nevertheless, he felt a deep connection with his fellow Jews. If a snail sheds its shell, he said, it's still a snail. Likewise, without the external trappings of religion, he was still a Jew.

THE NOBEL PRIZE

Fortunately, Einstein was in great demand all over the world. That got him out of Germany on speaking tours around Europe, Asia, the Middle East, and South America. In his travels, he lectured about relativity, and he raised funds for Zionism and other humanitarian causes.

During a 1922 trip to Shanghai, China, Einstein received word that he had won the 1921 Nobel prize for physics. It honored him "for his services to theoretical physics and in particular for his discovery of the law of the photoelectric effect." Although relativity had become his most famous concept, it was still too new and controversial for most scientists to accept. He gave the prize money he received to Mileva.

In spite of his success, Einstein was still discontent. Just as before, he felt that he had not taken relativity far enough. He was obsessed with finding a way to explain everything about matter and energy in one neat formula. This came to be called the unified field theory. However, neither Einstein nor anyone else has ever come up with such a theory.

PLAYING DICE WITH THE UNIVERSE

It aggravated Einstein that he could not figure out why light sometimes behaves like a particle and sometimes like a wave. Other scientists devised some answers to the particle-wave question and moved ahead to develop the field of **quantum mechanics**. One of its basic ideas was the uncertainty principle—the idea that one could never predict when an atom would release a quantum of light. Einstein could never accept this. "I cannot believe that God would choose to play dice with the Universe" was his now-famous comment.

opposite: Einstein at his home in Berlin in 1925

Science moved on, however, and quantum mechanics led to many revolutionary inventions. Einstein, for instance, had shown that light could be amplified. Further research in quantum mechanics produced the laser, a name that stands for "light amplification by stimulated emission of radiation." Now lasers have thousands of practical uses in medicine and industry.

opposite: The brilliant scientist maintained a healthy sense of humor.

Einstein's Scientific Humor

Einstein had a sense of humor about science, as shown by these statements:

- *Put your hand on a hot stove for a minute, and it seems like an hour. Sit with a pretty girl for an hour, and it seems like a minute. That's relativity!*

- *The only reason for time is so that everything doesn't happen at once.*

- *If the facts don't fit the theory, change the facts.*

- *Science is a wonderful thing if one does not have to earn one's living at it.*

- *If we knew what it was we were doing, it would not be called research, would it?*

- *Gravitation cannot be held responsible for people falling in love.*

- *If A equals success, then the formula is: A = X+Y+Z. X is work. Y is play. Z is keeping your mouth shut.*

- *The wireless telegraph is not difficult to understand. The ordinary telegraph is like a very long cat. You pull the tail in New York, and it meows in Los Angeles. The wireless is the same, only without the cat.*

CHAPTER 6

NEW HOME, OLD CONCERNS

Edwin Hubble, an astrophysicist with whom Einstein often shared his ideas, at the Mt. Wilson observatory

In 1930, Einstein began spending his winters at the California Institute of Technology in Pasadena, California. He especially enjoyed seminars at Mt. Wilson Observatory, where he met with astrophysicists Georges Lemaître and Edwin Hubble. The three laid the groundwork for the **big bang theory**, which proposes that the Universe began with a single explosion of densely concentrated mass and energy.

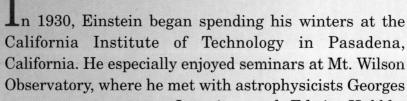

LEAVING GERMANY

Meanwhile, in Germany, Adolf Hitler was rising to power as the head of the Nazi Party, which was founded in 1919. His goal for the Nazi Party was to obtain German superiority over what he believed to be inferior races, including Jews, Slavs, and other non-German peoples. Soon after he became German chancellor in 1933, Hitler began to destroy the constitution and build a dictatorship. The Nazi Party seized control of Germany's courts, schools, newspapers, and police. People who opposed the government were beaten, imprisoned in concentration camps, forced to leave Germany, or murdered. In 1933, all German Jews were removed from government jobs, and within two years the rights of all Jewish citizens were revoked. From the beginning, Hitler turned anti-Semitism into an official government policy. Jewish scientists and scholars were special targets, since Hitler saw them as ringleaders of a Jewish conspiracy. Faced with this persecution, more than half of Germany's 500,000 Jews left the country.

In 1933, the Institute for Advanced Studies in Princeton, New Jersey, offered Einstein a professorship. As he saw little hope of surviving in Germany, he accepted the position. Shortly thereafter, he renounced his German citizenship. As a result, the Nazis seized Einstein's property and placed his name on a list of people whose citizenship had been stripped from them.

Einstein liked his new home in Princeton. "I have settled down splendidly here," he said. "I hibernate like a bear in its cave, and really feel more at home than ever before in my life." The Einstein household consisted of Albert, his wife Elsa, and his private secretary, Helen Dukas. Einstein's sister, Maria, moved in with them in 1939 and stayed until her death in 1951.

Adolf Hitler, German dictator and leader of the Nazi Party, in 1937

Einstein with Helen Dukas, his devoted secretary

German troops during their invasion of Poland in 1939

RUMORS AND WARNINGS

Germany's aggression worried Einstein. He thought war had become a thing of the past, but he was wrong. In 1939, Germany invaded Poland and World War II began. From other European scientists, Einstein began to hear frightening rumors. It seemed that Hitler's physicists had succeeded in splitting the nucleus of a uranium atom—the key event in making an atomic bomb.

The peace-loving scientist felt responsible. Such a weapon was a natural outgrowth of his own work. When the uranium atom was split, it lost mass, and that mass was released as an explosion of tremendous energy. Einstein was not at all pleased to know that this confirmed his formula $E = mc^2$.

He wrote a letter to President Franklin D. Roosevelt in 1939 to warn him about the Germans' research and about the massive destruction an atomic bomb could cause. He suggested that Roosevelt might begin thinking about conducting similar research.

Einstein on War

- *We are dealing with an epidemic delusion which, having caused infinite suffering, will one day vanish and become a monstrous and incomprehensible source of wonderment to later generations.*
- *My pacifism is an instinctive feeling, a feeling that possesses me because the murder of men is disgusting. My attitude is not derived from any intellectual theory but is based on my deepest antipathy to every kind of cruelty and hatred.*
- *I know not with what weapons World War III will be fought, but World War IV will be fought with sticks and stones.*

President Franklin D. Roosevelt was urged by Einstein to conduct research for creating atomic weapons.

Einstein Writes to Roosevelt

An excerpt from Einstein's August 2, 1939, letter to U.S. president Franklin D. Roosevelt:

Some recent work by E. Fermi and L. Szilard, which has been communicated to me in a manuscript, leads me to expect that the element uranium may be turned into a new and important source of energy in the immediate future. Certain aspects of this situation which has arisen seem to call for watchfulness and, if necessary, quick action on the part of the Administration. I believe therefore that it is my duty to bring to your attention the following facts and recommendations:

In the course of the last four months it has been made probable—through the work of Joliot in France as well as Fermi and Szilard in America—that it may become possible to set up a nuclear chain reaction in a large mass of uranium, by which vast amounts of power and large quantities of new radium-like elements would be generated. Now it appears almost certain that this could be achieved in the immediate future.

This new phenomenon would also lead to the construction of bombs, and it is conceivable—though much less certain—that extremely powerful bombs of a new type may thus be constructed. A single bomb of this type, carried by boat and exploded in a port, might very well destroy the whole port together with some of the surrounding territory. However, such bombs might very well prove to be too heavy for transportation by air.

The United States has only very poor ores of uranium in moderate quantities. There is some good ore in Canada and the former Czechoslovakia, while the most important source of uranium is Belgian Congo.

In view of this situation you may think it desirable to have some permanent contact maintained between the Administration and the group of physicists working on chain reactions in America. . . .

THE BOMB

Einstein had no idea of the effect his letter would have. In December 1941, when Japan bombed the U.S. naval base at Pearl Harbor, Hawaii, the United States entered the war. While the Germans surrendered in May 1945, conflicts still raged with Japan in the Pacific.

A cloud of smoke over Hiroshima, Japan, after the atomic bomb was dropped in August 1945

Meanwhile, in the six years since Einstein's 1939 letter, U.S. engineers had been conducting the top-secret Manhattan Project. Its mission was to develop an atomic bomb. On August 6, 1945, the first U.S. atomic bomb struck the city of Hiroshima, Japan, killing more than 140,000 people. Three days later, a second bomb was dropped on the city of Nagasaki, where 70,000 people were killed. Within days, Japan surrendered and the war was over.

CHAPTER 7

A PEACEFUL END

After World War II, Einstein spent much time at home and worked toward a world government.

War had only made Einstein a more ardent pacifist. In 1946, he became chairman of the Emergency Committee of Atomic Scientists. Its goal was nuclear disarmament and the control of nuclear energy. Einstein and other prominent U.S. citizens also campaigned for a "Federal Constitution of the world, a working legal worldwide order." He was sure that some kind of world government could prevent another world war.

opposite: An image of a black hole, one of the many phenomena that Einstein considered in the Universe

Taking Responsibility

In the *Bulletin of Atomic Scientists*, Einstein clearly stated the scientist's responsibility in preventing nuclear war:

We scientists, whose tragic destiny has been to help make the methods of annihilation ever more gruesome and more effective, must consider it our solemn and transcendent duty to do all in our power in preventing these weapons from being used for the brutal purpose for which they were invented.

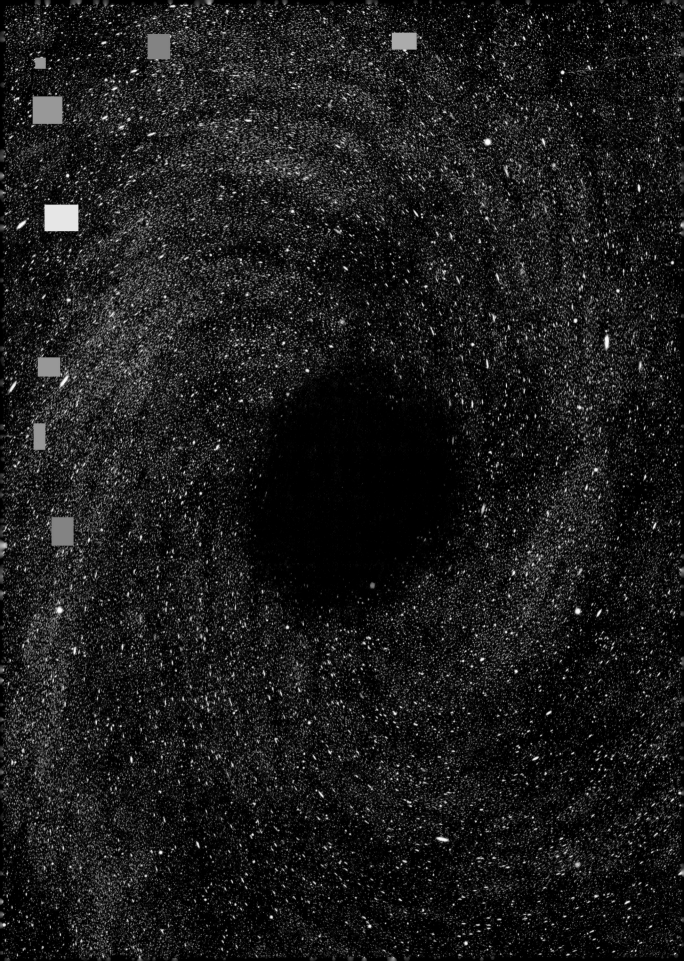

Einstein and his sister, Maria, continued to spend a great deal of time together in their later years.

opposite: All his life, Einstein enjoyed playing the violin.

As he grew older, Einstein became more interested in cosmology, which is the study of the Universe as a whole. He was pleased to see that physicists were coming to accept the big bang theory. It was a good explanation for why galaxies in the Universe were flying ever farther apart. Other scientists were applying his general theory of relativity to propose bold new possibilities—such as black holes (collapsed stars from which nothing escapes), **wormholes** (tunnels through space-time), and another universe parallel to our own.

FAMILY MATTERS

Einstein turned seventy in 1949, and his health was beginning to decline. His wife, Elsa, had died in 1936, and her daughter Margot took over many of her duties. Along with Einstein's secretary, Margot helped run the household, organize Einstein's mess of papers, and maintain the popular scientist's privacy.

Mileva, Einstein's first wife, lived until 1948. Their son Hans Albert had become an engineer and a professor of hydraulics at the University of California in Berkeley. Edward did not fare as well. For many years, the young man had been sick, and at one point, he was diagnosed with schizophrenia. Eventually, he was hospitalized and remained in an institution for the rest of his life.

Einstein's sister, Maria, still lived with him. After she suffered a stroke, he read to her every night. A friend described the siblings as "these two old people sitting together with their bushy hair, in complete agreement, understanding and love."

When he was at leisure, Einstein enjoyed sailing on Princeton's Lake Carnegie. He still enjoyed music, with Mozart as his special favorite. On walks with Margot, an artist and sculptor, the two shared a deep love of nature. People around Princeton easily spotted the gentle old scientist, with his unruly white hair sticking up in all directions. He refused to wear socks, and he lumbered along lost in scientific thoughts.

A HOME AT LAST

In 1948, the territory of Palestine was divided into Jewish and Arab sections. The portion designated for Jews became the State of Israel. Einstein was deeply satisfied to know that Jewish people at last had a homeland.

Always an advocate of human rights, Einstein had also campaigned for Arabs' rights in the division.

Einstein on Religion

Although Einstein did not believe in the traditional Judeo-Christian God, he sometimes spoke of God or a supreme being he called *Der Alte* ("The Old One"). Here are some of Einstein's thoughts on religion and ethics:

- *Science without religion is lame; religion without science is blind.*

- *A man's ethical behavior should be based effectually on sympathy, education, and social ties and needs; no religious basis is necessary. Man would indeed be in a poor way if he had to be restrained by fear of punishment and hope of reward after death.*

- *My religiosity consists in a humble admiration of the infinitely superior spirit that reveals itself in the little that we, with our weak and transitory understanding, can comprehend of reality. Morality is of the highest importance—but for us, not for God.*

opposite: Late in his life, Einstein was frequently seen walking around the Princeton campus.

When the presidency of Israel opened up in 1952, Israel offered the position to Einstein, its longtime friend and champion. He declined the offer. By now he was old, tired, and sick, and he relished the peace of his Princeton home.

Albert Einstein died on April 18, 1955, a month after his seventy-sixth birthday. The cause of death was an aortic aneurysm—the abnormal swelling of a major artery—that burst. His body was cremated, and the ashes were scattered in a secret location.

According to Einstein's wishes, his brain was saved for research. After examining it in 1955, a pathologist announced that there was nothing unusual about the brain. Scientists took another look in 1999. They found that it was missing a certain little wrinkle and that

regions on each side of that spot were enlarged. They were the inferior parietal lobes, associated with visual imagery and mathematical thinking.

No details of anatomy, however, can explain the man of compassion and simplicity who summed up his own life this way: "I am happy because I want nothing from anyone. I do not care for money. Decorations, titles, or distinctions mean nothing to me. I do not crave praise. The only thing that gives me pleasure, apart from my work, my violin, and my sailboat, is the appreciation of my fellow workers."

opposite: Einstein at his home in 1951 with David Ben-Gurion, the prime minister of Israel

The word of Albert Einstein's death was front-page news all over the world.

TIMELINE

1879	Albert Einstein is born on March 14 in Ulm, Germany
1896	Enters Zurich Polytechnic in Switzerland
1900	Receives his diploma from Zurich Polytechnic
1902	Begins working at the Swiss Patent Office in Bern
1903	Marries Mileva Maric
1905	In his "miracle year," publishes papers on molecular activity, light quanta, and his special theory of relativity
1914	Moves to Berlin; World War I begins
1916	Publishes his general theory of relativity
1918	World War I ends
1919	Einstein divorces Mileva and marries Elsa Löwenthall; the theory of relativity is proven; Einstein becomes world famous
1922	Receives the 1921 Nobel prize for physics
1933	Is appointed professor at the Institute for Advanced Study in Princeton and settles permanently in the United States
1936	Einstein's wife Elsa dies
1939	Einstein writes to U.S. president Franklin D. Roosevelt about atomic weapons; World War II begins
1940	Einstein becomes a citizen of the United States
1945	The United States drops atomic bombs on Hiroshima and Nagasaki, Japan; World War II ends
1946	Einstein serves as chairman of the Emergency Committee of Atomic Scientists
1952	Is offered the presidency of the state of Israel; he declines
1955	Dies on April 18 in Princeton at the age of seventy-six

anti-Semitism: hostility toward and discrimination against Jews

atom: the basic unit of matter

big bang theory: a theory in astronomy suggesting that the Universe originated billions of years ago in a single explosion

black hole: theoretically, a collapsed star so dense that nothing can escape its gravitational field

electrons: particles that carry negative electricity

lasers: from the phrase light amplification by stimulated emission of radiation, devices that produce very powerful beams of light; lasers are used for a variety of applications, including reading price codes, printing documents, repairing damaged eyes, and guiding missiles to a target.

light-years: units used by astronomers to describe the distance to and between stars; one light-year is the distance traveled in one year by a pulse of light; since light travels at 186,282 miles (299,792 kilometers) per second, one light-year equals about 5.88 trillion miles (9.46 trillion kilometers)

mass: the measure of how hard an object resists a change in speed or a change from still to moving; in simplified terms, mass means weight

molecules: the smallest units of a substance; composed of one or more atoms

Nobel prize: any of the annual prizes established by Alfred Nobel to encourage work in the interest of humanity; prizes are given for peace, literature, chemistry, medicine, physics, and economics

pacifist: one who supports peace and opposes war or violence

paradox: a situation that seems contradictory or contrary to common sense

photoelectric effect: the emission of electrons when light strikes a sheet of metal

photons: atomic particles that carry radiant energy; new name devised for Einstein's light quanta

physics: the study of matter and energy

quanta: small packets of radiant energy (heat or light); singular is quantum

quantum mechanics: the study of the behavior of atomic particles, involving matter and energy

relativity: how different objects are related to one another

space-time continuum: a four-dimensional field whose dimensions are length, width, height, and time

wormholes: theoretically, tunnel-shaped black holes connecting two regions in the space-time continuum

TO FIND OUT MORE

BOOKS

Bernstein, Jeremy. **Albert Einstein and the Frontiers of Physics**. New York: Oxford University Press Children's Books, 1997.

Cwiklik, Robert. **Albert Einstein and the Theory of Relativity**. New York: Barrons Juveniles, 1987.

Goldenstern, Joyce. **Albert Einstein: Physicist and Genius**. Berkeley Heights, N.J.: Enslow, 2001.

Hammontree, Marie. **Albert Einstein: Young Thinker**. Minneapolis: Econo-Clad Books, 1999.

MacPherson, Stephanie Sammartino. **Ordinary Genius: The Story of Albert Einstein**. Minneapolis: Carolrhoda Books, 1997.

Severance, John B. **Einstein: Visionary Scientist**. New York: Houghton Mifflin, 1999.

INTERNET SITES

Einstein: Image and Impact
http://www.aip.org/history/einstein/index.html
A complete survey of Einstein's life and work, from the American Institute of Physics.

Nobel e-Museum
http://www.nobel.se/
To learn more about the Nobel prize and all its recipients.

NOVA Online: Einstein Revealed
http://www.pbs.org/wgbh/nova/einstein/
Explores Einstein's discoveries about light, time travel, relativity, and the Universe as a whole.

Person of the Century: Albert Einstein
http://www.time.com/time/time100/poc/ magazine/albert_einstein5a.html
Essays on Einstein as *Time* magazine's Person of the Century.

INDEX

About the Author

Ann Heinrichs grew up in Fort Smith, Arkansas. She began playing the piano at age three and thought she would grow up to be a pianist. Instead, she became a writer. Now she has written more than fifty books for children and young adults. Several of her books have won national awards. Ms. Heinrichs now lives in Chicago, Illinois. She is a prize-winning martial artist, specializing in t'ai chi empty-hand and weapons forms, and enjoys traveling to Third World countries.

3112 (27)